A Walk Thru the Life of

SOLOMON

Pursuing a Heart of Integrity

Walk Thru the Bible

BakerBooks

a division of Baker Publishing Group
Grand Rapids, Michigan

© 2009 by Walk Thru the Bible

Published by Baker Books
a division of Baker Publishing Group
P.O. Box 6287, Grand Rapids, MI 49516-6287
www.bakerbooks.com

Printed in the United States of America

Library of Congress Cataloging-in-Publication Data
A walk thru the life of Solomon : pursuing a heart of integrity / Walk Thru the Bible.
    p.   cm.
   Includes bibliographical references.
   ISBN 978-0-8010-7174-4 (pbk.)
   1. Solomon, King of Israel. 2. Bible. O.T. Kings, 1st—Study and teaching.
3. Bible. O.T. Kings, 1st—Criticism, interpretation, etc. I. Walk Thru the Bible
(Educational ministry).
BS580.S6W37 2009
222′.53092—dc22   2008050824

Cover image: Lili Boas / iStock

Contents

Introduction

It started with a man, then a family, then a clan, then an entire ethnic group. But the day the people of Israel walked out of Egypt and passed through a sea, they became a nation. They tried having God as their only king, but everyone did what was right in their own eyes and didn't serve him. Then, in a bad case of royal envy, they cried out for a human king, and they got what they asked for. Eventually, the kingdom was ripped out of the bad king's hands and given to a man after God's own heart—a passionate warrior/poet/musician/shepherd/king. And finally, the king with a heart built a kingdom with a heart—and a promise of everlasting glory.

Israel was a small country at the end of David's reign, but it was a country with an enormous purpose and a godly king. The twelve tribes had been united, the territory solidified, the military established, the enemies subdued, the priests assigned, the worship cultivated, and the temple imagined. And this was no ordinary kingdom; there were eternal promises associated with it and a global influence to come. This wasn't just a nation chosen to prosper. It was chosen to host the presence of God.

That's the remarkable legacy Solomon inherited—Israel was a jewel in God's crown and the delight of his eyes. During the course of Solomon's reign, this unique treasure would rise to unprecedented heights and then, almost inexplicably, begin to fragment into tragic rivalries. While Solomon was king, the world saw both what it was like for a nation to be blessed by God and what it was like for a nation to betray that sacred trust. Sadly, the legacy he left was less righteous than the legacy he received, and the holy inheritance would slip through the grasp of generations to come.

Solomon the King

Solomon reigned over a united kingdom from 967 to 927 BC. He was the third king of Israel and, in many ways, a strange hybrid between the first two. The first king, Saul, had no heart for the Lord. The second, David, had a whole heart for the Lord. And the third, David's son, had a divided heart. He loved the Lord and followed in David's footsteps, but he hung onto his baser desires and eventually departed from his father's path.

Solomon was the second son of David and Bathsheba—the first died in infancy as God's judgment on David's sin of taking Bathsheba from her husband and having him killed in battle. But Bathsheba remained David's most beloved wife, and Solomon was his most beloved child. He grew up as a son of privilege and was taught by his father to love the Lord—an experience he wrote about in Proverbs 4:3–9:

> When I was a boy in my father's house, still tender, and an only child of my mother, he taught me and said, "Lay hold of my words with all your heart; keep my commands and you will live. Get wisdom, get understanding; do not forget my words or swerve from them. Do not forsake wisdom, and she will protect you; love her, and she will watch over you. Wisdom is

supreme; therefore get wisdom. Though it cost all you have, get understanding. Esteem her, and she will exalt you; embrace her, and she will honor you. She will set a garland of grace on your head and present you with a crown of splendor."

Those are words to live by, which is exactly what Solomon did for much of his life. But he wasn't consistent in following his own advice. He forgot those words, ignored them, or intentionally rebelled against them at times, and the consequences were painful. Late in life, he became bitter, disillusioned, lethargic, depressed, and apathetic.

The biblical information we have on Solomon comes from 1 Kings 1–11 (the primary narrative for this study); 2 Chronicles 1–9; Proverbs; Ecclesiastes; and Song of Songs. The passages from Kings and Chronicles are written about him in the third person, while much of Proverbs was written and compiled by him. Ecclesiastes does not name its author, but internal evidence points to Solomon. And he is associated with the Song of Songs in its first verse.

Themes

The story of this king has a noticeable symmetry. With a humble heart, he inherited a great kingdom from his father, displayed remarkable wisdom from God, governed a glorious period of growth and prosperity, was recognized for his glory, was lavishly honored for his wisdom, and then left a broken kingdom to his son. It's the story of a rise and fall, of wisdom and foolishness, of God's kingdom and human kingdoms, and of power and weakness. Solomon is a complex character in whom the ups and downs common to all of us are magnified to epic proportions. He's a valuable case study in how to obey God and how not to obey God; in one way or another, he represents the best and worst of who we are.

Important themes and lessons to watch for in Solomon's life include:

- priorities in prayer
- priorities in personal decisions
- knowing truth versus doing truth
- power, wealth, and ambition
- how God disciplines his people
- the conditional nature of many of God's promises
- the privileges and responsibilities of being chosen by God
- principles of leadership
- living by principles versus living from a changed heart
- integrity

How to Use This Guide

The questions in this guide are geared to elicit every participant's input, regardless of his or her level of preparation. Obviously, the more group members prepare by reading the biblical text and the background information in the study guide, the more they will get out of it. But even in busy weeks that afford no preparation time, everyone will be able to participate in a meaningful way.

The discussion questions also allow your group quite a bit of latitude. Some groups prefer to briefly discuss the questions in order to cover as many as possible, while others focus only on one or two of them in order to have more in-depth conversations. Since this study is designed for flexibility, feel free to adapt it according to the personality and needs of your group.

Each session ends with a hypothetical situation that relates to the passage of the week. Discussion questions are provided, but group members may also want to consider role-playing the scenario or setting up a two-team debate over one or two of the questions. These exercises often cultivate insights that wouldn't come out of a typical discussion.

Regardless of how you use this material, the biblical text will always be the ultimate authority. Your discussions may take you to many places and cover many issues, but they will have the greatest impact when they begin and end with God's Word itself. And never forget that the Spirit who inspired the Word is in on the discussion too. May he guide it—and you—wherever he wishes.

A Fruitful Legacy

1 KINGS 1–2

On the surface, he had it all. He was high-profile royalty: wealthy, educated, influential, supported by powerful people, and very, very handsome. And he was the oldest among his brothers, a prince among princes. He thought his time had surely come.

But Adonijah's time hadn't come—at least not the time he had expected. No, he had assumed that since his father's health was failing, it would be expedient to go ahead and pursue both the throne and enough backing to make sure he could hold it. After conferring with a powerful general and a well-placed priest, it seemed the plan would work. The barely-coherent king would certainly appreciate and agree to a peaceful succession in which all the details had already been worked out.

11

Adonijah invited key members of his constituency—royal courtiers and tribal leaders of Judah and Benjamin, his father's power base—to a nearby spring and made ceremonial sacrifices to ask God's blessing on his kingship. The ensuing feast would solidify the new king's alliances.

But someone forgot to tell the king—that is, until the prophet Nathan and the king's beloved wife Bathsheba realized what was happening. They immediately hatched a plan to solicit David's favor for Solomon, his son with Bathsheba. It was this son, not the oldest one, who had been called "beloved by God" (2 Sam. 12:24–25). It was this son to whom David had promised the throne. So the old king named Solomon his successor, ordered the ceremonial entry into Jerusalem on a mule, and invited Solomon to sit on his throne amid trumpet blasts and shouts of acclamation. The retinue would include the high priest, a high general, and foreign mercenary troops. The coronation would be much more official, if not more popular, than Adonijah's feast at the spring.

LIKE FATHER, UNLIKE SON

Solomon's rise to the throne of Israel was sudden. His father's, however, took years. David was anointed king long before Saul died; their rivalry resulted in David's exile and Saul's relentless pursuit. David refused to force his way into his position, even when he had a golden opportunity to kill the reigning king. And the conflict extended beyond Saul's death. "The war between the house of Saul and the house of David lasted a long time" (2 Sam. 3:1), as the tribes of Israel wrestled with the decision of whether to follow David or a son of Saul. Eventually, of course, God established David as king. And as is often the case, a father's long labor gives his son an advantage. Solomon only had to fight for the throne for a day.

SHALOM

When the Bible speaks of peace, it means more than simply the absence of conflict. The Hebrew word *shalom*—related to Solomon's name (*Shelom*oh) and the name of Jerusalem (Yeru*shalaim*)—also includes fulfillment, wholeness, completeness, safety, and abundance. It's an "all is well" satisfaction with life—exactly what Solomon will describe in 5:4: "The Lord my God has given me rest on every side, and there is no adversary or disaster." Under Solomon, the kingdom of Israel will experience *shalom* for the first and perhaps only time in its history.

In less than a day, Adonijah went from almost-king to almost-executed. Through the maneuverings of an inner circle of king's allies, Israel made its first transition of power from a father to son. And the nation entered its golden age.

Power plays are almost always messy, even when they involve divinely chosen people and a sovereign God. Solomon's birth itself came in the aftermath of a mess; he was the product of a marriage that only happened because David stole a man's wife and had the man killed. It's one of those examples of how God redeems our lives, even when we've done a royal job of messing them up. The years we've wasted aren't actually a waste in his economy.

Conspiracies: 1 Kings 1

Focus: 1 Kings 1:24–31

The palace intrigue involved in Solomon's ascent to the throne hints of two stories from Genesis: (1) the rivalry between Cain and Abel, in which only one brother could live; and (2) the rivalry between Jacob and Esau, in which only one brother could inherit the father's blessing. Between Solomon and Adonijah, only one brother can assume the throne and, as it turns out, survive the competition. For all of the posturing and oaths of protection, Adonijah's threat remains. He even flaunts it, requesting his father's consort in an attempt to hold on to some claim to the throne (2:13–25). So yet another of David's sons dies in the heat of a bitter rivalry, and only one is left standing in the bloody mess: Solomon the wise.

Though Solomon is lauded for most of the biblical account of his life, a dark side of his reign is foreshadowed early in the narrative. Neither a prophet of God nor the king's favorite wife nor the king's beloved son is immune from the seduction of power. The kingdom's welfare must be, of course, their primary concern; but just as prominent should be concern for survival and the influence they can have. Not only does Solomon gain the throne; he also eliminates those who threaten his right to it. The kingdom he acquires has come at a cost.

Discuss

- Which aspects of Solomon's ascension seem godly? Which seem ungodly? Do you think God would have established him on the throne without the power play? Why or why not?

  _____

  _____

  _____

  _____

- Solomon was the eventual fruit of David's worst moral failure—his relationship with Bathsheba—and a clear indication that God can use our messes as integral aspects of his plan. Do you feel as if any part of your life has been wasted? If so, how might God redeem those parts for his purposes?

_____

_____

_____

_____

_____

_____

Promises: 1 Kings 2

Focus: 1 Kings 2:1–4

As David nears death, he gives his son a solemn charge: walk according to God's commands as put forth in the books of Moses, and live with wholehearted faithfulness. Why? So that Solomon will prosper and so that God's promises to David of a perpetual dynasty will be fulfilled.

God's promises for a lasting dynasty had been given to David years before because of his undivided heart. But they were conditional on the behavior of his descendants. Even in his dying words, David seems to realize that. His legacy won't be fulfilled if his children's hearts don't remain pure. And to this point in his parenting experience, things have not gone well. Sons have rebelled, brothers have killed brothers, and only one hope is still standing.

David's last instructions for Solomon are the lens through which his reign will be assessed. When Solomon succeeds, it will be because he has lived up to his father's words. And when Solomon fails, as the writer of 1 Kings will show us, it will be because he has abandoned them.

15

Discuss

- How would you feel if you knew the fulfillment of God's promise to someone else depended entirely on you? Would the responsibility to fulfill someone else's conditions be more likely to have a positive or negative effect on you? Why?

  _____
  _____
  _____
  _____

- Do you think it's possible for parents to pass a pure heart down from one generation to the next? Why or why not? If so, how?

  _____
  _____
  _____
  _____

A CASE STUDY

Imagine: He was a young candidate, but after a long history of corrupt presidents, youth was an asset. It gave him the appearance of innocence. And in his case, it was more than an appearance. He was idealistic, visionary, optimistic, and unstained by the ugly effects of under-the-table deals and cutthroat politics. He was a new and promising face.

Naturally, he was elected, mainly because everyone loves a new face. And the first two years of his term went remarkably well. But in the third year, a scandal surfaced—the first of many. The honeymoon was over. Illegal fundraising, deceptive claims, and destroyed reputations would mark the rest of his presidency. Power, it seems, corrupted even the most promising of careers.

- Is it possible for a leader to increase in both power and faithfulness at the same time? Why or why not?
- Why do power and success seem to corrupt even pure hearts?
- Does this situation apply only to kings and presidents, or have you noticed the corrupting influence of authority in your circles of friends and associates? What can a person do to remain humble and pure in the midst of great or sudden success?

The Wisdom of the Lord

1 KINGS 3–4

With most kings, they wouldn't have even received a hearing. They were prostitutes, after all; there's no guarantee they would have even been heard by the lowest court. But this particular case was no property dispute. It had a particular poignancy. Two illegitimate babies were born in the same disreputable household, and one died. Both women claimed the child who lived—a son who might one day provide for an old adulteress even when no one else would. The king's judgment would determine whether the child would be raised by its mother or a heinous liar.

On the surface, the king's decision was shockingly absurd. Dividing the child in half would ensure a miscarriage of justice. The mother would be deprived of her child, the child

GOOD ADVICE OR IRON-CLAD GUARANTEES?

Solomon "spoke three thousand proverbs and his songs numbered a thousand and five" (4:32). Some of that prolific output is recorded in Proverbs, Ecclesiastes, and the Song of Songs, but much of it is lost in antiquity. The book of Proverbs, in particular, most of which was written and compiled by Solomon, contains the wisdom spoken of in 1 Kings.

But what kind of wisdom is it? Many Christians read Proverbs as a collection of hard-and-fast promises and then are shocked when a gentle answer, for example, doesn't turn away wrath (15:1). (It's comforting to know that gentle answers didn't always spare Jesus, the disciples, or Paul from the wrath of their opponents either.) It can also be alarming when the righteous don't live a long life and the wicked do (see 10:27); or when humility and the fear of the Lord don't seem to bring much wealth and honor (22:4). Many Proverbs are general principles for the normal practice of life, and many must be recast as promises for eternity rather than the here and now. Regardless, these wise sayings are inspired by God for a reason: to lead us in right paths.

would be deprived of its life, and the liar would have lost nothing. But the decision was a ruse, a test to bring out the truth. A real mother would be willing to give up her child to anyone rather than see him die. And she'd say so with an impassioned plea.

This story is perhaps the best-known incident of Solomon's reign. It makes a dramatic point that true wisdom seeks truth more than an efficient decision. It falls short of demonstrating true justice; the liar gets no punishment or even rebuke. And there's a lot more practicality than compassion in it. Still, the truth is revealed, and a mother receives back her child.

This kind of wisdom is rare in any era, including our own. Court systems often focus on legalities at the expense of truth.

After all, discovering the truth of a situation takes time and interest. Many people don't have either.

That applies not only to court systems but also to the details of interpersonal relationships. Practicing wisdom requires some sort of investment—of thought, of time, of emotion. Mostly it requires a discerning spirit and dependence on the God who has all understanding and has promised to share it.

Back to Egypt: 1 Kings 3:1–3

The first statement after the kingdom is "firmly established" in Solomon's hands foreshadows one of his greatest flaws. He marries a foreign wife, an Egyptian princess, in order to strengthen his alliance with (and reliance on) his powerful neighbor to the south. God's law prohibited such marriages for Israel's kings— not because God is opposed to foreigners in Israel, but because of the temptation it would bring. God knows the influence of a wife, and an idolatrous influence in the royal household could end in disaster.

SOLOMON'S MODEL PRAYER

Solomon's encounter with God in a dream is a model prayer and a powerful case study on the principle Jesus articulated in Matthew 6:33: "Seek first his kingdom and his righteousness, and all these things will be given to you as well." Not coincidentally, Jesus referred to Solomon only a few sentences before that statement (Matt. 6:29). It's a familiar passage on trusting God for the material necessities and blessings of life, and it seems that the worry-free lilies of the field had an advantage over Solomon in all his splendor. The king's security didn't come without stress; the lilies' security—and ours, if we'll trust—can.

21

In fact, Solomon demonstrates an affinity for Egypt throughout his reign. He adopts Egyptian administrative units for his government, trades for Egyptian horses and chariots, and establishes Egyptian labor policies. All were warned against long ago in Israel's history, but Solomon doesn't heed those warnings. Figuratively, he takes Israel, whose national identity was birthed when it was delivered from slavery in Egypt, back to the land of its oppressor. This is not a good sign.

Discuss

- In what ways do we tend to "rely on Egypt"—to depend on tangible security instead of on God—in our lives? What sources of provision and protection other than him do we tend to seek? How difficult would it be to give up some of these false dependencies?

  _____

  _____

  _____

  _____

- What is your primary source of wisdom? How well do you adhere to the wisdom you receive?

  _____

  _____

  _____

  _____

A Holy Moment: 1 Kings 3:4–15

Solomon travels to Gibeon, the site of the most significant national altar, in order to make sacrifices and seek the favor of

God. As pilgrims often do, he spends the night in the presence of the altar in order to give God an opportunity to speak to him in a dream. His hope is realized. In the first of two landmark visitations in his life, God gives him an astounding offer: "Ask for whatever you want me to give you." In a model prayer, Solomon nobly chooses wisdom, which results in God granting him over and above his request. In addition to a discerning heart, he gets riches, honor, and a long life.

Discuss

- To what degree do your prayers reflect the priorities of Solomon's prayer?

  _____

  _____

  _____

  _____

- Ephesians 3:20 tells us that God can do far more than we can even ask or think. Have you ever experienced God's "above and beyond" answers to your prayers? If so, what are some examples?

  _____

  _____

  _____

  _____

Kingdom Come: 1 Kings 4:20–21, 25, 29–34

In many ways, the description of Solomon's kingdom at its prime is a picture of the kingdom of God in its fullness. There's abundant provision, safety, and peace according to the promises of Torah (Lev. 26:3–13, for example). First Kings 4:25 even points to a common picture of the messianic age: the citizens of Israel each sitting under their own fig tree (also Mal. 4:4).

The problem is that while there is great efficiency in the well-functioning systems in Solomon's realm, there's not much reference to the character of the king or his people. They are enjoying the fruits of God's wisdom and law, but are they fully committed to his ways? Are they in sync with his heart?

It's interesting that these verses of great prosperity raise plenty of issues between the lines. As 1 Kings will make clear, this kingdom has been built with some dependence on Egyptian and Phoenician resources and expertise, forced labor, and heavy taxes. It has became prosperous, but at a cost. In fact, part of the cost has come in how the nation now measures success: the standard for comparison is with "the other nations" (4:29–34). Israel, the chosen nation that was set apart to the Lord and given a distinct role and divine revelation, is beating its neighbors at their own game.

Discuss

- What would "heaven on earth" look like to you? How closely does it match the description of Solomon's kingdom in 1 Kings 4?

_____

_____

_____

_____

24

A CASE STUDY

Imagine: The church was primed for growth. There were plenty of people serving in key roles, plenty of space, and plenty of motivation among its members to grow. The problem? Growth wasn't happening. Not yet. And no one was quite sure why.

That's when the leadership team decided to hire a marketing consultant to develop a new image for the congregation and a business consultant to develop more efficient processes and programs. The result would be plenty of changes, though no one knew what kind or how much. Would there be a turnover in staff? A different style of music? Another burdensome capital campaign? New interior decorating? Or even a move to a new facility in another part of town?

- In what ways can a desire for effective ministry cause us to compromise our principles?
- In Romans 12:2, Paul says not to be conformed to the pattern of this world. In 1 Corinthians 9:22, he says he has become all things to all men in order to save some. Where should a church draw the line between these two principles? Where should an individual believer draw that line?
- Which of the world's practices and attitudes do you think the church as a whole is most tempted to imitate? Which are easiest to distance ourselves from?

The Glory of the Lord

1 KINGS 5–8

Hudson Taylor was brokenhearted over China, so much so that he left everything behind in England and devoted his life to evangelizing the vast nation's interior. Plenty of Christians in England came to admire his life of faith. Others questioned the integrity of British colonialism. It was, after all, "the imperial century," the era when great European powers scrambled to snap up territory in the Americas, Asia, and Africa. The British emerged victorious among lesser powers and became the world's largest empire. It was a golden age of expansion, commerce, prosperity—for many. But it was a hard age for African tribes and Asian subjects. There were blessings, to be sure, the greatest of which was an open door for Christian missions. But there were curses too as Christianity was the furthest thing from

27

SOLOMON'S PALACE

The temple, his father's dream, took seven years to build, and Solomon's palace took nearly twice that long. So which project did Solomon personally value more? The temple (built first) or the palace (built bigger)? Interestingly, the thirteen-year period of palace construction fits neatly into anyone's theory. Those who believe Solomon valued the temple more highly argue that he dragged his feet on the palace because he was less zealous about it. Those who think he valued the palace more argue that he spent those long, painstaking years because he was more zealous about it. And those who don't think there's enough evidence to determine Solomon's priorities have the simplest argument: the palace took longer because it was bigger.

many colonialists' minds. The empire was driven by progress and paternalism, faith and power, good works and greed. It was a very mixed bag.

So it is with the kingdom of God in any era. God uses Roman oppressors and colonial governments to open doors for the gospel, but he doesn't endorse everything those governments do. More personally, we may walk in very unworthy ways at times in our lives, yet he guides our steps to put us in places of fruitfulness (Prov. 16:9). The dreams and ambitions of our hearts blend with the desires and purposes of his heart, and the result is a joint venture with our heavenly Father.

How does he work through such obviously earthen vessels? He doesn't tell us the exact mechanics of that synergy, only that it exists. He not only tolerates it, he designed it. Why? Because he's a God of relationships. He made us in his image in order to fill us with himself. His plan has always been to dwell among us.

Shalom for a Season: 1 Kings 5:3–5, 13–18

David's dream was to build a temple for the Lord, but that dream was denied by God because of all the blood the king had shed. God did, however, promise David that his son could build the temple. So now in a time of *shalom*, which his father never experienced on a national scale, Solomon begins to carry out David's desire.

Because of the king's skill at foreign relations and international trade, he is able to obtain the finest materials from abroad. But the labor he procures from within Israel is conscripted or "forced" (5:13–14). Three shifts of ten thousand men rotate on a monthly basis, each group having one month on and two months off. The system is efficient and productive, but it won't be without controversy in the long run. Israel fled the slavery of Egypt's construction projects long ago; Solomon is the first king to suggest that perhaps God's people should again be forced to build the nation's buildings.

PRAYING FROM DEUTERONOMY

Solomon's prayer of dedication will sound very familiar to those acquainted with Deuteronomy. It uses a lot of the same phrases and terms: "there is no God like you," "a covenant of love," heaven as God's "dwelling place," the land as an inheritance. Because of that connection, the temple dedication can be seen as a fulfillment of Deuteronomy's promises—and also a reiteration of its warnings. The covenant is reaffirmed, with all its blessings for obedience and consequences for the lack thereof. And at the moment of Solomon's prayer, Deuteronomy's blessings are manifestly real.

Discuss

- There's a clear connection in 1 Kings between Israel's time of peace and the temple of God's presence. What connection is there in your life between peace and his presence? What can you do to cultivate times of experiencing his presence more?

  _____

  _____

  _____

  _____

  _____

Construction and Instruction: 1 Kings 6:11–13

In the middle of the temple project, the word of the Lord comes to Solomon again. This isn't quite on the level of the epiphany he experienced at Gibeon; a vision in chapter 9 is considered the second of his divine encounters. But the timing of this message from God is significant. It reiterates the words of David's charge at the beginning of Solomon's reign, but the conditions are emphasized. "*If* you follow my decrees, carry out my regulations *and* keep all my commandments *and* obey them, [*then*] I will fulfill through you the promise I gave to David your father" (6:12). And verse 13 warns how high the stakes are: the conditions will make the difference between God's presence and his abandonment.

Discuss

- Do you think the dynamics between Israel and God—specifically their faithfulness as a necessary condition for his manifest presence—apply to the church today? Why or why not?

_____

_____

_____

_____

_____

Jerusalem Crowned: 1 Kings 8

Focus: 1 Kings 8:10–12, 27–30, 56–61

After the completion of the temple in seven years, Solomon builds a palace for himself (chapter 7), and it takes him thirteen years to do it. The entire building plan raises the beauty and prestige of Jerusalem to unprecedented heights. And when all the articles of worship are prepared and the temple is fully embellished, the time for dedication coincides with the Feast of Tabernacles, a celebration with heavy connotations of the ultimate fullness of God's kingdom.

The temple dedication is lengthy—even more so in the 2 Chronicles version—as the ark of the covenant is installed in the Holy of Holies, a cloud of glory fills the building, Solomon prays an extensive blessing and prayer, and a multitude of sacrifices are offered. One of the most encouraging lines in Scripture anchors that ceremony: "Not one word has failed of all the good promises he gave through his servant Moses" (8:56). By the time the feast ends and the vast assembly departs, the nation is "joyful and glad in heart for all the good things the Lord had done for his servant David and his people Israel" (8:66).

The prayer of dedication the people have recently heard was full of both the blessings and the dangers of God's presence. Being called by him has enormous benefits and enormous costs.

31

The cloud of glory that filled the temple was both beautiful and frightening. These are the two sides of chosenness: amazing privilege and awesome responsibility. The king will soon feel the sharpness of this two-edged calling. Before long, so will the entire nation.

Discuss

- What are some of the blessings of being chosen by God? What are some of the responsibilities? Is it possible for believers to experience one without the other? Why or why not?

  _____

  _____

  _____

  _____

  _____

A CASE STUDY

Imagine: A bright light and a voice from heaven wakes you up in the middle of the night. You immediately know it's the Lord, and he offers you an amazing choice between two very real alternatives. You can choose to experience his powerful, overwhelming presence in and around you, knowing that you will experience incredible responsibility and hardship, but the burden will be far outweighed by incredible blessing and honor. Or you can go on living in the status quo—a normal, uninterrupted life just like most of the people around you. Whatever you choose, there will be no guilt involved; either is acceptable to the Lord. But you have to choose one or the other.

- Which would you choose and why?
- From what you know of human nature, which alternative do you think most people would prefer? Why?
- In what respects is this scenario an actual choice we have to make? What are the costs involved in experiencing God's presence? What are the benefits?

The Wisdom of Solomon

1 KINGS 9

Greg had prayed for God's blessings and favor when he got out of college, and God had certainly answered. Greg had been given a beautiful family, and his career had taken off dramatically. He rose from entry level to executive in the short space of seven years, and people in the industry began calling him flattering things like "wunderkind" and "prodigy." He had proven himself capable beyond his peers and wise beyond his years.

So Greg began to lead seminars and write books about the keys to his success. His already-generous income more than doubled from his international speaking fees. He became widely recognized as a "how to" expert, a motivator, and a life coach. A few bestsellers later, his family was able to buy several homes in several countries. He was credited with more talent and

TEMPLE TRUST

Long after Solomon ruled, God's dire warnings against idolatry in 9:6–9 were about to be realized. The prophets foretold a coming invasion by Babylon if the nation didn't repent—an invasion that would eventually result in the total destruction of Jerusalem and the temple. Jeremiah's indictment against trusting in the temple was particularly sharp: "This is what the LORD Almighty, the God of Israel, says: Reform your ways and your actions, and I will let you live in this place. Do not trust in deceptive words and say, 'This is the temple of the LORD, the temple of the LORD, the temple of the LORD!' " (Jer. 15:3–4). The people had assumed that the temple ensured God's presence, and God's presence ensured protection. Meanwhile, they worshiped false gods, shed innocent blood, and oppressed the weakest members of society. They forgot a principle that's just as relevant today as it was then: religious props are no substitute for heartfelt obedience to God.

skill and ingenuity than anyone around. Yes, he was truly a self-made man.

But self-made men eventually suffer the consequences of poor construction, and a series of misfortunes left Greg virtually bankrupt. His books ended up in bargain bins, his seminars were suddenly "cliché," and his family hardly knew the man who had always been too busy to spend time with them. And Greg found himself exactly where he began when he was fresh out of college: on his knees asking for God's blessings and favor.

It's a common dynamic, isn't it? We ask God for help, and he gives it. The Holy Spirit fills us with himself, and then we take credit for his gifts. Once we experience success, whether in the big-ticket items like career and family or the smaller victories of life, we develop a sense of independence. We start patting ourselves on the back for being so competent or wise or well-positioned. And then when our mini-kingdom crumbles, we fall on our knees again and ask God for help.

Solomon began his reign with a sincere plea for God's wisdom and favor. Somewhere along the way, that sense of dependence began to erode. The turning point in the text, although there were earlier signs, seems to be after the temple and palace were built. A focus on God's glory seems to have evolved into a focus on Solomon's glory. And things were never the same again.

Promises—with Warnings: 1 Kings 9:1–9

Early in his reign, Solomon heard God's voice at Gibeon. Now he hears it again—a similar message, but this time with much stronger warnings. There are far more "ifs" in this vision, as well as some explicitly stated consequences for idolatry. God assures Solomon that worshiping other gods will ruin Israel's relationship with him, and the place of his presence would be demolished. It's clear that the temple itself won't guarantee the

THE EVERLASTING KING?

God had promised David an everlasting legacy of messianic proportions. So when Solomon proved to be a wise king who extended Israel's borders, presided over the nation's longest era of peace, built a temple for God's presence, established Jerusalem as a praise in the earth, and amassed an enormous reservoir of wealth, it seemed that God's promise had been fulfilled in the first generation after it had been given. Few expected the King of Peace to fall and the kingdom to divide, and even fewer suspected that the everlasting King and the age of fulfillment would come after many centuries of grief, judgment, and oppression.

spiritual maturity of his people. The current presence of the Lord doesn't guarantee his future presence.

This warning isn't just a precautionary safeguard. It's a rather timely admonition. The glory of Solomon's kingdom has begun to overshadow his sense of dependence. He is in danger of self-sufficiency, which always creates distance in a relationship with God. The warning he receives reminds him that God's people are not defined by a magnificent building, even one in which God's presence dwells. They are defined by his calling and his Word. Only when they stick to truth will they be blessed.

Discuss

- The prophets often portrayed our relationship with God as a marriage and our idolatry as adultery. In what ways is that idea expressed in this passage? How might this marriage illustration apply to current attitudes about tolerance and diversity?

  _____

  _____

  _____

  _____

  _____

- Why is our self-sufficiency so offensive to God that he would strip us of all that supports us and makes us feel secure? Have you seen him do that in your experience?

  _____

  _____

  _____

  _____

  _____

Efficiency Expert: 1 Kings 9:10–14, 20–22

Solomon's kingdom-building continues with great success. He wheels and deals with the king of Tyre, constructs the walls of Jerusalem, builds and/or rebuilds several cities, and strengthens his military. He's not only a king, he's an entrepreneur. He blends the expansion of the kingdom of God with the expansion of his own influence, and enough is never enough.

But Solomon loses some support in his ambitious undertakings by conscripting laborers from his own people. Whether this amounts to slavery or not—9:22 says no, while 5:13–14 and 12:4 clearly indicate that the labor has been forced—it is enough to make Israel feel burdened under the weight. A restlessness develops that will one day, after Solomon is gone, create political turmoil for his son and spark division in the kingdom. In the psyche of the nation, this forced labor is like the anti-Exodus. It takes the chosen people emotionally back to Egypt.

Discuss

- As part of our salvation, we're set free from the things that once held us captive. In what ways do we tend to "go back to Egypt"? What happens to us spiritually when we do? How can we avoid doing this?

_____

_____

_____

_____

A Case Study

Imagine: Your best friend has it all together. She brings home a great income, she has her children running like clockwork, her house is spotless, and she seems to have plenty of time to hang out with friends such as you. You've asked her how she does it, and she has responded with a multitude of quips and quotes and life principles that make it sound so simple. But over time, you become aware of some underlying problems. Her kids and her husband feel neglected—their resentment is almost but not quite suppressed—and in honest moments of your conversations, you can tell she isn't really satisfied. Her happy life isn't quite as happy as it appears.

- Why is a smooth-functioning personal life so desirable to us? Why is it not enough to make us happy?
- If you could pick three things to arbitrarily change about your personal, day-to-day lifestyle, what would they be? How would those changes make your life better?
- Is it possible to train yourself in a set of Christian principles and then live simply by habits and disciplines? Why or why not?

The Glory of Solomon

1 KINGS 10

The torch lit up the courtyard, giving it an almost haunting beauty—a warm glow on the walls, flickering shadows dancing across the ground. Moths darted around it, unable to keep their distance, almost daring the flame to burn them. And the guests, alive with conversation and contentment, flocked to its radiance. It created an irresistible atmosphere.

That's God's design for drawing people to himself. It began with a single promise to one man. The divine voice was clear: "You are chosen, and the whole world will be blessed through you." That was Abraham's first encounter with God (Gen. 12:1–3), but it wouldn't be his last. In fact, the voice would

A PICTURE OF JESUS

Many Christian Old Testament scholars see Solomon as a type of Christ—a picture of the King to come. His fame and glory and wealth foreshadow the glories of the kingdom of God as described in the New Testament, especially Revelation. His reign brings peace. The building of the temple comes with promises of God's eternal presence with his people and hints at the kind of worship we'll offer around the heavenly throne. And his wisdom points to Jesus, who became God's wisdom for us (1 Cor. 1:30). But types can only anticipate the real thing, not match it. Jesus was clear that "one greater than Solomon is here" (Matt. 12:42).

come to his descendants again and again and again, often delivering a variation on the same message. "He will set you in praise, fame and honor high above all the nations he has made," it spoke to another generation (Deut. 26:19). The Creator's purpose was plain: all of creation would flock to him.

We see the fulfillment of that promise in Revelation 5:11, as every creature sings out: "To him who sits on the throne and to the Lamb be praise and honor and glory and power, for ever and ever!" But in between Abraham and heaven, we get lots of other glimpses of the promise. As Solomon's kingdom shone with the glory of God like a flame that lights up the world, people were drawn to it. They offered their gifts and their compliments without restraint.

This is also God's desire for us—to be drawn to him like a moth to a flame, like common nations to a kingdom of glory, like hearts trying to find their true home. A greater King than Solomon is raised up to the throne, and those who really see him find him irresistible.

Light for the Nations: 1 Kings 10:1–13

The queen of Sheba, a kingdom at the southwest corner of the Arabian peninsula and the horn of Africa, makes a diplomatic visit to Israel and gives Solomon a lot of diplomatic compliments. But the praise she lavishes on his kingdom goes well beyond diplomacy. She is, to say the least, impressed. And the text is clear that she relates the glory of this kingdom not only to Solomon but to the God of Israel. She tests Solomon's reputation with hard questions, sees his wealth with her own eyes, praises him and his Lord for such favor, and offers him extravagant gifts. Like many other nations, she is drawn to the light. Solomon, in return, gives her "all she desired and asked for" (10:13). It's a graphic picture of how God answers prayers and bestows blessings on those who worship him.

TRANSGRESSIONS

Though 1 Kings 10 reads as a glowing account of Solomon's reign, a Torah-observant Jew would notice some alarming facts in the chapter. The instructions of Deuteronomy 17 are clearly ignored: "The king, moreover, must not acquire great numbers of horses for himself or make the people return to Egypt to get more of them, for the Lord has told you, 'You are not to go back that way again.' He must not take many wives, or his heart will be led astray. He must not accumulate large amounts of silver and gold" (Deut. 17:16–17). Isaiah 31:1 contains an even stronger warning: "Woe to those who go down to Egypt for help, who rely on horses, who trust in the multitude of their chariots and in the great strength of their horsemen, but do not look to the Holy One of Israel, or seek help from the Lord." Though Isaiah came much later than Solomon, his warning comes straight out of Deuteronomy—and indicates a frequent neglect of the law by Israel's kings that began with Solomon.

A dramatic tension for Israel throughout its biblical history is whether it will fulfill its calling to be a light to the nations. Will it be an influencer of nations? Or will it be influenced by them? For the most part, the record isn't very positive. In 1 Samuel, it asks for a king so it can be like the other nations. Its kings often made treaties with other nations, trusting in the same horses and chariots that God said he didn't need. And Solomon, as we've noted, had a certain taste for all things Egyptian. At the same time, however, Israel had been set apart and, in very significant ways, would always be distinctive.

Discuss

- What do you think makes a member of the kingdom of God different than the rest of the world? In what ways do we sometimes try to minimize those distinctives?

  _____

  _____

- What evidence of light has God used to draw you closer to him?

  _____

  _____

Golden Days: 1 Kings 10:14–29

Solomon acquires only the finest materials for his kingdom. He is an importer/exporter of expensive goods, and he uses them in every aspect of his government. Ample gold goes into the equipment for both the palace and the military. The choicest horses and chariots are imported to strengthen the army, with plenty left over for export to potential enemies. The extravagance is unprecedented.

Because of the glory of the kingdom—and because such glory is generally considered evidence of the favor of the gods—people come from all over the known world to hear the wisdom God put into Solomon's heart. And they don't come empty-handed. Knowing the value of the wisdom they will receive, their natural inclination is to bring gifts.

The opulence of Solomon's kingdom raises an interesting question. Is he a snapshot of the Lord who reigns over a more impressive kingdom from an even more extravagant throne—his kingdom being a portrayal of the age to come? Or is he a dramatic warning against materialism and greed? The biblical text implies that his wealth is from God's favor, yet the description of it will flow right into an explanation of his downfall. Apparently, the blessings of God come with a heads and a tails: the greater the benefits, the greater the responsibility of stewarding them. And in stewarding them, Solomon has clearly forgotten some of his own proverbs about the deceitfulness of wealth, the beauty of simplicity, and the transparency of fame. He is, in many ways, a wise fool.

Discuss

- What is your initial reaction to Solomon's extravagance? Is it a blessing or a character flaw? Why?

  _____

  _____

- What is your initial reaction to any Christian ministry that basks in wealth? Why?

  _____

  _____

A Case Study

Imagine: You live in a culture characterized by its sophistication, education, self-sufficiency, diversity, tolerance, economic development, and global trade. Within that culture is a community of faith that is generally very knowledgeable about Scripture yet very unwilling to heed some of its main teachings. As a result, the community of faith blends in with the larger culture to a significant degree. On a foundation of biblical values, entrepreneurship, and extraordinary ambition, the nation has grown stronger than all those around it. But the compromises of those values and the relentlessness of that ambition have created a cultural time bomb. Some experts even envision a disastrous collapse on the horizon.

- Do you think our society today is similar to the kingdom under Solomon? If so, how?
- To what extent do you think the church is driven by consumerism? To what extent are you?
- How is it that many Christians can know the Bible inside and out yet still not live out its principles? In what ways have you felt pressure to compromise with the culture around you?

A Futile Legacy

1 KINGS 11

Hamartía. It's the tragic flaw of a main character in a Greek play, the hubris of a literary hero, and the New Testament word for sin. In Solomon's case, it was all of the above—and more. Legends and fairy tales are formed from such character flaws. So, in this case, was history.

The Solomon of chapter 3 was a model of humility, a youth who knew his youthfulness, a dependent in an over-his-head situation. So he humbly and nobly beseeched the Lord for the wisdom he would need as ruler of the people of God. Now near the end of his reign, he has somehow lost sight of his need for guidance and grown complacent in his satisfaction. It was a sudden change; he had married the Egyptian princess soon after his father died (3:1) and an Ammonite even before David's death (see 14:21). The

STILL ON BESTSELLER LISTS

Usually when a well-known leader publicly confesses his serious moral failures, he steps down from his ministry and his books drop off the bestseller lists. That isn't the case with Solomon who, in spite of the Bible's very frank assessment of his sins, continued to be revered throughout scriptural history and is still idealized today. And his writings? As part of the Bible, they continue to top the best-seller lists. We zealously study the maxims of someone who didn't follow them.

That raises a perplexing issue: God apparently speaks inspired truth through servants whom he knows will later discredit it. Yet the message is still valid—God inspired Proverbs, after all—even though the messenger seems to have been exposed as a fraud. So how should we regard the ministry of a minister who falls? Is his fruit from God or not? When is a leader's failure a sign of hypocrisy, and when is it a sign of understandable flaws? These are hard questions that will always be relevant when flawed human beings handle divinely inspired words.

roots of his sin went way back, but they were overshadowed by his practical wisdom. Somewhere, somehow, the wisdom faded, at least in practice, and the folly ran rampant. Why?

"Pride goes before destruction," Solomon had once written (Prov. 16:18). He also wrote that "when pride comes, then comes disgrace, but with humility comes wisdom" (Prov. 11:2). Those words would be strangely prophetic in his case; he fulfilled them all. Perhaps his wisdom and wealth cultivated pride—it has to be hard to keep your humility when people keep telling you how unimaginably gifted you are—and pride did the ugly work he said it would. Regardless, he somehow missed the connection between his instructions and his application. He was a great observer of human nature and terrible example of it at the same time. He lived a life of massive contradictions.

That's what pride does; it blinds. Every human being needs affirmation, but when we get so much of it that we lose sight of our weaknesses, we tend to ignore God. We need him in our desperation. When everything's fine, we take the wheel. And Solomon steered in some very dangerous directions.

Money, Sex, and Power: 1 Kings 11:1–13

"King Solomon, however, loved many foreign women." Thus begins the account of the end of the golden age. The scriptural prohibition against this practice of intermarriage has little to do with the fact that the women are foreign and everything to do with the fact that they are idolaters. Perhaps they were required to formally convert to Judaism at the time of their marriage, but Solomon allows them to retain their old ways of worship. He tolerates their pagan altars. He brings impurity into the land of promise.

THE CHRONICLES DIFFERENCE

The book of 2 Chronicles also tells of Solomon's reign, using much of the same content as 1 Kings, but it is written from a different perspective. Whereas 1 Kings relates issues relevant to both the northern and southern kingdoms, 2 Chronicles tells only the history relevant to Judean kings and events and keeps the story very, very positive. It gives a greatly expanded description of the temple dedication, for example, and avoids negative reporting, never describing Solomon's contentious coronation or mentioning his foreign wives and idolatry. Because there are many added insights and well-known verses in the account, it's worth reading as a different slant on Solomon's life.

Solomon is more than a philanderer. He's a shrewd political strategist. His marriages aren't just about love but about sealing alliances with fellow kings. His thirst for expansion causes him to compromise biblical instruction, and the compromise eats away at his heart. In his old age, he turns away from God. In one of the most radical downfalls in Scripture, he worships at the shrine of a Phoenician goddess and an Ammonite god. Worship of the former often involved decadent fertility rituals, and worship of the latter often involved particularly painful infant sacrifices by burning. Even indirect association with such deities is repulsive to God. But Solomon's heart, not fully devoted to begin with (11:4), is invested in women who worshiped them. That leads him to do evil in the sight of the Lord (11:6).

Solomon's marriages are a graphic picture of divided loyalties, a physical portrayal of a spiritual truth. Just as one man can't possibly love all those women, one person can't love a multitude of gods. But Solomon tries to embrace every loyalty, thereby becoming ultimately disloyal. What seemed like a mostly pure heart in chapter 3 turns out to be a very divided heart in the end. And the nation becomes a mirror image of its leader: divided and disloyal.

Discuss

- Do you think Solomon knew he was disobeying God's law in his marriages, alliances, and dependence on foreign resources? Why do you think he forgot or ignored his own wisdom in these matters?

  _____

  _____

  _____

  _____

- In what areas do you forget or ignore the wisdom you've already learned?

  _____

  _____

  _____

  _____

All Is Vanity: 1 Kings 11:26–39

God raises up rivals against Solomon because of his sin. He had warned of such consequences, and now they are coming to pass. But God's promises to David included an intact kingdom under his son's reign, so he preserves a remnant to remain loyal to Solomon. The rest of the kingdom, however, will fall into the hands of a God-called, prophet-endorsed rebel. The northern ten tribes will become "Israel" while Solomon's remnant becomes "Judah." The judgment will be painful—but not forever.

We know from the rest of the passage that Solomon tried to kill Jeroboam just as Saul had pursued David. And in a twist of irony, Jeroboam escapes to Solomon's ally Egypt. We also know from the book of Ecclesiastes that Solomon became an embittered, pessimistic old man who realized the futility of the human experience apart from God. The elder Solomon has quite a jaded view of money, sex, and power; they aren't enough to satisfy. He becomes bored and depressed.

Discuss

- Augustine wrote that our hearts are restless until they find their rest in God. Blaise Pascal wrote that we all have a God-shaped hole in our hearts. What did Solomon try to fill his God-shaped hole with? What have you tried to fill yours with? Why do so many attempts to fill ourselves leave us feeling so empty?

_____

_____

_____

_____

A Case Study

Imagine: The minister sat in his study with the door firmly closed and, though everyone had gone to bed hours ago, securely locked. Part of him hated himself for what he was viewing on his computer screen; he had always heard that temptation will come at leaders with money, sex, and power, and he knew which area was his weakest. But in other ways, he could easily rationalize his visual exploration. After all, he wasn't actually indulging in any specific biblical sin—he couldn't think of a chapter and verse anyway—and he had never committed blatant immorality himself. Compared to many men, he had very high morals. And isn't it important for people who minister to the world to understand how people think and to be able to relate to their temptations? Plus, he was bored with life and tired from its struggles. *I know there are better ways to ease my stress,* he admitted to himself. *I'll try to think of some tomorrow.*

- Is this scenario more shocking or less shocking to you than Solomon's indiscretions? Why?
- How has this person exalted his own rationale over and above the wisdom of God? In which areas of life do you dilute God's wisdom with your own preferences?
- What do you think is the root cause of ignoring God's wisdom? How does the gospel fix a heart in that condition?

Conclusion

From glory to vanity, Solomon's life has been an enigma. The king who began his reign in wisdom, love for God, obedience, and prosperity has finished his reign in foolishness, love for women, disobedience, and brokenness. The golden age of Israel serves as a model of the kingdom of God and points us to his desire to bless and strengthen us and to shine in a way that all the world see him. And the end of the golden age serves as a harsh reminder of how negligence and apathy toward God results in futility. For Solomon, prosperity—both the material and spiritual kind—was dangerous. For us, it's a blessing with a sharp edge.

Solomon's father once appointed a worship leader named Asaph to minister before the ark of the covenant. He was, in a sense, the minister of music in the tabernacle of David. Asaph's declaration to the Lord in Psalm 73:25 would have served Solomon well: "Whom have I in heaven but you? And earth has nothing I desire besides you." When Solomon desired God above all, God gave him all. When Solomon desired power, wealth, and women above God, God took all away. God was no longer his priority.

Perhaps that's the primary theme of Solomon's life: priorities. He's a case study in how God responds to right and wrong priorities as well as an example of how priorities can subtly shift over time. When we understand the issues he faced and the ways he faced them, we're led to reorder our priorities according to God's purposes. Our heart is to match his heart, not just for a season of our lives, but the whole way through.

Leader's Notes

Session 1

If there's time, the sidebar article "Like Father, Unlike Son" may be used to spark a discussion on how to tell the difference between times to wait in faith for God to move you and times to act decisively in faith to follow God's promise. David waited when he had opportunities to act; Solomon, at David's instructions, acted immediately to pursue the promise of kingship. The life of faith is full of this tension between waiting and acting. Participants will likely have a variety of experiences and opinions to share.

Session 3

This session makes the point that "God uses Roman oppressors and colonial governments to open doors for the gospel, but he doesn't endorse everything those governments do." If desired, you can prompt further discussion by inviting participants to think of how that statement applies to current governments. In what ways, for example, has the global economy—often fueled by consumer excesses and corporate abuses—allowed Christians to further the gospel? Group members can probably think of several examples that highlight the tension caused by God doing his work through flawed human beings and institutions. Ideally, this should lead into some discussion of personal application—specifically, how we can best carry out the kingdom mission while avoiding the cultural/political/economic baggage that often accompanies it.

Session 5

A Case Study. This scenario shouldn't be very hard for participants to imagine. It's a fairly accurate description of American culture and the church's position in it. The discussion will undoubtedly touch on some relevant themes and specific experiences of members. Wherever possible, it may be helpful to encourage personal examples.

Session 6

A Case Study. This situation may be uncomfortable for some participants to read, but according to statistics, it's a reality for many in today's Christian culture. This description of it is designed to capture the incongruence of Solomon's life and the staggering nature of his fall. In fact, though its immediacy might shock us more, a minister with an addiction is much less of a fall than someone who has been endowed with God's own wisdom worshiping at a gruesome site of child sacrifices because some women in his harem convinced him to. That's the stunning picture of Solomon's decline.

Bibliography

Alexander, David, and Pat Alexander. *Zondervan Handbook to the Bible*. Grand Rapids: Zondervan, 1999.

Berlin, Adele, Marc Zvi Brettler, and Michael Fishbane, eds. *The Jewish Study Bible*. Oxford and New York: Oxford University Press, 2004.

Brueggemann, Walter. *1 Kings*. Louisville: John Knox, 1982.

Chilton, Bruce, et al. *The Cambridge Companion to the Bible*. Cambridge and New York: Cambridge University Press, 1997.

Dumbrell, William J. *The Faith of Israel: A Theological Survey of the Old Testament*. Grand Rapids: Baker Academic, 2002.

Shanks, Herschel, ed. *Ancient Israel: From Abraham to the Roman Destruction of the Temple*. Upper Saddle River, NJ: Prentice Hall, 1999.

Telushkin, Joseph. *Biblical Literacy: The Most Important People, Events, and Ideas of the Hebrew Bible*. New York: William Morrow, 1997.

Walton, John H., Victor H. Matthews, and Mark W. Chavalas. *The IVP Bible Background Commentary: Old Testament*. Downers Grove, IL: InterVarsity Press, 2000.

Wilkinson, Bruce, and Kenneth Boa. *Talk Thru the Old Testament*. Nashville: Thomas Nelson, 1983.

**WALK
THRU THE
BIBLE**

Helping people everywhere
live God's Word

For more than three decades, Walk Thru the Bible has created discipleship materials and cultivated leadership networks that together are reaching millions of people through live seminars, print publications, audiovisual curricula, and the Internet. Known for innovative methods and high-quality resources, we serve the whole body of Christ across denominational, cultural, and national lines. Through our strong and cooperative international partnerships, we are strategically positioned to address the church's greatest need: developing mature, committed, and spiritually reproducing believers.

Walk Thru the Bible communicates the truths of God's Word in a way that makes the Bible readily accessible to anyone. We are committed to developing user-friendly resources that are Bible centered, of excellent quality, life changing for individuals, and catalytic for churches, ministries, and movements; and we are committed to maintaining our global reach through strategic partnerships while adhering to the highest levels of integrity in all we do.

Walk Thru the Bible partners with the local church worldwide to fulfill its mission, helping people "walk thru" the Bible with greater clarity and understanding. Live seminars and small group curricula are taught in over 45 languages by more than 80,000 people in more than 70 countries, and more than 100 million devotionals have been packaged into daily magazines, books, and other publications that reach over five million people each year.

Walk Thru the Bible
4201 North Peachtree Road
Atlanta, GA 30341-1207
770-458-9300
www.walkthru.org

Read the entire Bible in one year, thanks to the systematic reading plan in the best-selling **Daily Walk** devotional.

The **Daily Walk** devotional magazine includes book introductions, charts outlining book and chapter themes, and background information on each day's reading. Insightful observations shed light on the culture, the history, and the context of passages. Each daily reading is loaded with helpful applications that enable you to apply biblical truth to your life. Readers are sure to find the time they spend in the Bible more productive and rewarding than ever before.

Ideal for church-wide or group Bible study, bulk subscriptions to **Daily Walk** offering significant savings can be purchased online at www.walkthru.org. Discounted individual subscriptions are also available online.

WALK THRU THE BIBLE

www.walkthru.org

11856521R10038

Made in the USA
San Bernardino, CA
30 May 2014